49 Arthritis Salad Recipes to Minimize Aches and Pains:

The Natural Solution to Your Arthritis Problems

By

Joe Correa CSN

COPYRIGHT

© 2019 Live Stronger Faster Inc.

All rights reserved

Reproduction or translation of any part of this work beyond that permitted by section 107 or 108 of the 1976 United States Copyright Act without the permission of the copyright owner is unlawful.

This publication is designed to provide accurate and authoritative information in regard to the subject matter covered. It is sold with the understanding that neither the author nor the publisher is engaged in rendering medical advice. If medical advice or assistance is needed, consult with a doctor. This book is considered a guide and should not be used in any way detrimental to your health. Consult with a physician before starting this nutritional plan to make sure it's right for you.

ACKNOWLEDGEMENTS

This book is dedicated to my friends and family that have had mild or serious illnesses so that you may find a solution and make the necessary changes in your life.

49 Arthritis Salad Recipes to Minimize Aches and Pains:

The Natural Solution to Your Arthritis Problems

By

Joe Correa CSN

CONTENTS

Copyright

Acknowledgements

About The Author

Introduction

Commitment

49 Arthritis Salad Recipes to Minimize Aches and Pains: The Natural Solution to Your Arthritis Problems

Additional Titles from This Author

ABOUT THE AUTHOR

After years of Research, I honestly believe in the positive effects that proper nutrition can have over the body and mind. My knowledge and experience has helped me live healthier throughout the years and which I have shared with family and friends. The more you know about eating and drinking healthier, the sooner you will want to change your life and eating habits.

Nutrition is a key part in the process of being healthy and living longer so get started today. The first step is the most important and the most significant.

INTRODUCTION

49 Arthritis Salad Recipes to Minimize Aches and Pains: The Natural Solution to Your Arthritis Problems

By Joe Correa CSN

Arthritis is a highly inflammatory disease that usually affects multiple joints in the body. Although there are around a hundred different types of this disease, two of the most common ones are:

- Osteoarthritis
- Rheumatoid arthritis

In most cases, both types of arthritis develop in adults over the age of 60. However, due to poor diet, lack of exercise, and excess weight, arthritis can also develop in children, teens, and young adults. Also, arthritis is more common in women than men.

Early symptoms of arthritis include joint pain, joint swelling, stiffness (especially in the morning), and redness of the skin around the affected joint. In most cases, symptoms don't develop overnight but over a long period of time (months or even years). Other common symptoms most people affected by arthritis often experience loss of appetite, energy loss, slight fever, and red blood cell count decrease. Recognizing the symptoms of arthritis and seeing the physician is an extremely important part of the treatment because both, osteoarthritis and rheumatoid arthritis can cause severe joint deformity if left untreated.

Osteoarthritis is caused by the reduction in the normal amount of cartilage tissue surrounding the joints. This reduction, furthermore, can be caused by normal wear, different infections, injuries, etc.

Rheumatoid arthritis, on the other hand, is an autoimmune disease of the synovium inside the joints. Although the exact cause of autoimmune diseases is unknown, rheumatoid arthritis occurs when our own immune systems attack the soft tissue in joints.

It is important to point out that both types of arthritis are directly related to the types of food we eat, body weight, and overall health. A healthy diet, anti-inflammatory foods loaded with healthy nutrients, fresh fruits and vegetables, plenty of good proteins and healthy carbs are the first step in preventing and treating both types of arthritis.

For this reason, I have decided to create this fantastic collection of arthritis preventing and curing salad recipes. Based on carefully selected ingredients, these salad recipes can easily replace your regular meal and find its place on your daily menu. They have the ability to cure your body and help you fight off this serious disease.

Enjoy every single one of them.

49 ARTHRITIS SALAD RECIPES TO MINIMIZE ACHES AND PAINS: THE NATURAL SOLUTION TO YOUR ARTHRITIS PROBLEMS

1. Smoked Salmon Salad

Ingredients:

4 oz. smoked salmon, sliced

½ red onion, sliced

1 cup Iceberg lettuce, roughly chopped

¼ cup Feta cheese, crumbled

¼ cup Kalamata olives, pitted

1 tbsp. extra-virgin olive oil

¼ tsp. garlic powder

½ tsp. dried thyme

¼ tsp. dried rosemary

¼ tsp. sea salt

¼ tsp. black pepper, ground

Preparation:

In a small bowl, combine olive oil, garlic powder, thyme, rosemary, salt, and pepper. Stir until well combined and set aside.

Rinse and drain the lettuce. Roughly chop and place in a large bowl. Top with onions, salmon, and cheese.

Drizzle with previously prepared dressing and serve immediately.

Optionally, sprinkle with some fresh lemon juice for some extra taste.

Enjoy!

Nutritional information per serving: Kcal: 213, Protein: 13.7g, Carbs: 5.9g, Fats: 15.4g

2. Spinach Mushroom Salad

Ingredients:

4 cups fresh spinach, rinsed

2 cups button mushrooms

1 medium-sized red onion, thinly sliced

3 tbsp. olive oil

1 tsp. coconut sugar

¼ cup balsamic vinegar

½ tsp. salt

¼ tsp. black pepper, ground

Preparation:

In a small skillet, combine balsamic vinegar, coconut sugar, salt, and pepper. Bring it to a boil and remove from the heat immediately. Let it chill completely and then add sliced onions. Cover with a lid and refrigerate for later.

Now, preheat the oil in a large skillet over medium-high heat. Add mushrooms and sprinkle with some salt and pepper to taste. Cook for 10 minutes, stirring occasionally.

Add one cup of spinach to the skillet and cook for 1-2

minutes, or until the spinach has been wilted. Remove from the heat and set aside.

Arrange the remaining spinach on a serving plate and top with mushroom and spinach mixture. Add onions and remaining marinade.

Serve immediately.

Nutritional information per serving: Kcal: 243, Protein: 4.6g, Carbs: 11.5g, Fats: 21.5g

3. Green Bean Salad with Baby Potatoes

Ingredients:

2 cups fresh green beans

1 cup baby potatoes, peeled

1 small red onion, sliced

3 tbsp. olive oil

2 tsp. yellow mustard

1 tsp. fresh thyme, finely chopped

2 tsp. lemon juice, freshly squeezed

¼ tsp. salt

¼ tsp. black pepper

Preparation:

In a small mixing bowl, combine olive oil, yellow mustard, thyme, lemon juice, salt, and pepper. Mix until well combined and set aside.

Place the green beans in a deep pot and add water enough to cover. Sprinkle with some salt and bring it to a simmer. Cook for 2-3 minutes, or until almost tender. Remove from the heat. Using a large mesh skimmer, transfer to a large bowl and set aside.

Place the potatoes to the same pot and bring it to a boil over medium-high heat. Simmer for 10-12 minutes, or until fork-tender. Remove from the heat and drain. Cut into bite-sized pieces and add to the bowl with green beans.

Add onions and drizzle all with previously prepared dressing. Gently toss until well incorporated and serve immediately.

Nutritional information per serving: Kcal: 246, Protein: 3.2g, Carbs: 14.3g, Fats: 21.5g

4. Frisee Arugula Salad

Ingredients:

3 cups fresh frisee, torn

2 cups arugula, torn

1 tbsp. lemon juice, freshly squeezed

1 tsp. Dijon mustard

1 tbsp. olive oil

½ tsp. salt

¼ tsp. black pepper, ground

½ tsp. Italian seasoning

Preparation:

Combine all greens in a large colander. Rinse under cold running water and drain. Chop into bite-sized pieces and transfer to a large bowl. Set aside.

In a small bowl, combine lemon juice, Dijon mustard, olive oil, salt, pepper and Italian seasoning. Mix until well combined and drizzle over the salad.

You can add some more greens of your choice, such as spinach, kale, or watercress. However, it's optional.

Serve immediately.

Nutritional information per serving: Kcal: 246, Protein: 3.2g, Carbs: 14.3g, Fats: 21.5g

5. Sweet Buckwheat Salad with Avocado and Spinach

Ingredients:

1 cup buckwheat groats

½ ripe avocado, peeled and sliced

1 cup fresh spinach, rinsed and chopped

½ medium-sized cucumber, sliced

½ cup black beans, soaked overnight

1 whole lime, juiced

1 tbsp. olive oil

1 tsp. maple syrup

¼ tsp. cumin powder

¼ tsp. cayenne pepper

Salt and pepper to taste

Preparation:

Place the buckwheat in a heavy-bottomed pot and add 2 cups of water. Bring it to a boil over medium-high heat. Cook for 10-15 minutes, or until tender. Remove from the heat and drain the excess liquid. Set aside.

Drain the beans and place them in a pot. Add water enough to cover all and bring it to a boil. Cook for 30 minutes. Remove from the heat and drain. Set aside.

Using a large colander, rinse the spinach under cold running water. Drain and transfer to a large bowl. Add cooked buckwheat, cooked beans, avocado, and sliced cucumber.

In a small bowl, combine olive oil, lime juice, maple syrup, cumin powder, cayenne pepper, salt, and pepper. Stir well until combined and drizzle over the salad.

Serve immediately.

Nutritional information per serving: Kcal: 287, Protein: 10.2g, Carbs: 38.1g, Fats: 12.2g

6. Fried Red Bell Pepper Salad

Ingredients:

5 medium-sized red bell peppers, halved lengthwise and seeds removed

1 garlic clove, minced

1 tbsp. capers, drained

¼ cup olives, pitted

1 tbsp. balsamic vinegar

2 tbsp. extra-virgin olive oil

1 tbsp. fresh parsley, finely chopped

1 tsp. sea salt

Preparation:

In a small bowl, combine garlic, capers, olives, balsamic vinegar, parsley, salt, and one tablespoon of oil. Stir well and set aside for 15 minutes before use.

Grease a large non-stick pan with the remaining olive oil. Heat up over medium-high heat. Add bell peppers and sprinkle with some salt. Cook for 5 minutes, or until tender and brown on the edges. Remove from the heat and transfer to a large bowl.

Top with previously prepared mixture and sprinkle with finely chopped parsley before serving.

Nutritional information per serving: Kcal: 240, Protein: 3.4g, Carbs: 24.5g, Fats: 16.6g

7. Cheesy Chicken Salad

Ingredients:

1 lb. chicken breast, skinless and boneless

¼ cup cottage cheese, crumbled

1 medium-sized red bell pepper, chopped

1 small cucumber, sliced

1 small red onion, chopped

2 cups Romaine lettuce, chopped

1 tsp. lemon juice, freshly squeezed

1 tsp. Worcestershire sauce

1 tbsp. olive oil

½ tsp. dried thyme, ground

¼ tsp. smoked paprika

¼ tsp. garlic powder

Salt to taste

Preparation:

Rinse well the chicken and pat-dry with a kitchen paper.

Transfer to cutting board and cut into bite-sized pieces. Set aside.

Preheat the oil in a saucepan over medium-high heat. Add chicken and sprinkle with garlic powder, thyme, smoked paprika, and salt to taste. Cook for 5-7 minutes, or until golden brown. Remove from the heat and set aside.

Rinse the lettuce under cold running water. Chop into bite-sized pieces and place in large bowl along with cottage cheese, cucumber, bell pepper, and onion.

Sprinkle all with Worcestershire sauce and lemon juice. Give it a good stir and serve immediately.

Nutritional information per serving: Kcal: 275, Protein: 36.2g, Carbs: 11.4g, Fats: 9.2g

8. Sweet Potato Salad with Eggs

Ingredients:

2 medium-sized sweet potatoes

2 eggs

1 medium-sized onion, sliced

1 tbsp. olive oil

1 tbsp. fresh parsley, finely chopped

½ tsp. salt

½ tsp. black pepper, ground

¼ tsp. dried oregano, ground

¼ tsp. dried rosemary, ground

Preparation:

Place the eggs in a deep pot and add enough water to cover. Bring it to a boil and cook for 10 minutes. Remove from the heat and transfer immediately to ice cold water. Let it chill for a few minutes. Peel and cut into bite-sized pieces. Set aside.

Peel the potatoes and cut into bite-sized cubes.

Peel the onion and cut into thin slices. Set aside.

Place the sweet potatoes in a heavy-bottomed pot and cover with water. Bring it to a boil and cook for 7-10 minutes over a medium-high heat. Remove from the heat and drain well.

Preheat the oil in a large saucepan over medium-high heat. Add potatoes and sprinkle with salt, pepper, oregano, and rosemary. Cook for 2-3 minutes and remove from the heat.

Transfer the potatoes to a large bowl along with eggs, onion, and parsley. Stir until well incorporated.

Nutritional information per serving: Kcal: 217, Protein: 5.7g, Carbs: 32g, Fats: 7.9g

9. Greek Style Salad

Ingredients:

2 large tomatoes, chopped

¼ cup Feta cheese, crumbled

1 cucumber, sliced

1 medium-sized capsicum, chopped

1 small onion, chopped

¼ cup black olives, pitted

1 tbsp. olive oil

½ tsp. salt

½ tsp. black pepper, ground

Preparation:

Rinse the tomatoes and transfer to a cutting board. Cut into bite-sized pieces and set aside.

Wash the cucumber and cut into thin slices. Set aside.

Peel the onion and chop into small pieces. Place in a small bowl and add water enough to cover. Sprinkle with some salt and mix. Let it soak for 10 minutes. When done, drain and squeeze with your hands to remove the excess water.

Wash the pepper and cut lengthwise into halves. Remove the stem and seeds. Chop into small pieces and set aside.

Now, combine all prepared ingredients in a large bowl. Add olives and sprinkle all with olive oil, salt, and pepper to taste. Give it a good stir and serve immediately.

Nutritional information per serving: Kcal: 209, Protein: 6.3g, Carbs: 20g, Fats: 13.5g

10. Cabbage Radish Salad

Ingredients:

2 cups cabbage, shredded

2 medium-sized radishes, thinly sliced

1 medium-sized purple onion, sliced

2 eggs

1 tbsp. olive oil

1 tbsp. white wine vinegar

1 tsp. Italian seasoning

¼ tsp. black pepper, ground

Preparation:

Wash the radishes and trim off the green parts. Using a sharp knife, cut into thin slices and set aside.

Peel the onion and cut into thin slices. Sprinkle with some salt and set aside.

In a small mixing bowl, combine olive oil, vinegar, Italian seasoning, and pepper. Mix until well combined and set aside.

Place the eggs in a deep pot. Add water enough to cover and bring it to a boil over medium-high heat. Cook for 10 minutes and remove from the heat. Let it cool completely. Peel and cut into bite-sized pieces.

Now, combine cabbage, radishes, onion, and eggs in a large bowl. Drizzle with previously prepared dressing and serve immediately.

Nutritional information per serving: Kcal: 173, Protein: 7.1g, Carbs: 10.2g, Fats: 12.2g

11. Mediterranean Salad

Ingredients:

4 oz. shrimps, cleaned and deveined

1 cup cherry tomatoes, halved

1 medium-sized purple onion, sliced

1 green bell pepper, chopped

¼ cup green olives, pitted

½ ripe avocado, sliced

¼ cup goat's cheese crumbled

2 tbsp. olive oil

1 tsp. balsamic vinegar

½ tsp. sea salt

¼ tsp. dried thyme, ground

¼ tsp. dried oregano, ground

¼ tsp. black pepper

Preparation:

Preheat one tablespoon of olive oil in a large non-stick

skillet over medium-high heat. Add shrimps and sprinkle with some salt and pepper. Cook for 2-3 minutes on each side. Remove from the heat and set aside.

In a small mixing bowl, combine the remaining olive oil, balsamic vinegar, thyme, and oregano. Mix until combined and set aside.

Wash and prepare the vegetables.

Now, combine shrimps, cherry tomatoes, purple onion, green bell pepper, and olives in a large salad bowl. Drizzle all with previously prepared dressing and gently toss.

Finally top with cheese and avocado slices and serve immediately.

Enjoy!

Nutritional information per serving: Kcal: 304, Protein: 14.8g, Carbs: 13.9g, Fats: 22.4g

12. Rice Vegetable Salad

Ingredients:

½ cup brown rice, long-grain

2 tbsp. olive oil

½ cup cherry tomatoes, halved

1 small cucumber, cut into bite-sized cubes

2 oz. Feta cheese, crumbled

½ tbsp. sherry vinegar

1 small onion, finely chopped

1 garlic clove, minced

½ cup fresh mint, roughly chopped

½ cup fresh parsley, roughly chopped

Salt and pepper to taste

Preparation:

Preheat one tablespoon of olive oil in a saucepan over medium-high heat. Add minced garlic and finely chopped onions. Sprinkle with some salt and stir-fry for 3-4 minutes, or until translucent. Remove the mixture from the pan and set aside.

Add the remaining oil to the pan and heat up over medium-high heat. Add rice and fry for 2 minutes, or until slightly golden brown. Pour in 1 ½ cup of water and stir well. Bring it to a simmer and reduce the heat to low. Cook for 25-30 minutes, stirring occasionally. Remove from the heat and cover with a lid. Let it sit for 5 minutes.

Now, combine rice and onion mixture in a large bowl. Add tomatoes and cucumber. Sprinkle all with sherry vinegar, salt, and pepper to taste. Optionally, add some olive oil for extra flavor.

Finally, stir in the cheese, mint and parsley.

Serve immediately.

Nutritional information per serving: Kcal: 287, Protein: 7.1g, Carbs: 34.5g, Fats: 14.6g

13. Creamy Beet Salad

Ingredients:

6 oz. beets

1 egg, hard-boiled

½ cup Greek yogurt

2 tbsp. sour cream

2 tsp. yellow mustard

1 tbsp. fresh parsley, finely chopped

1 garlic clove, minced

2 walnuts, minced

2 tsp. pumpkin seeds

1 cup fresh arugula, roughly chopped

1 tbsp. olive oil

Salt

Preparation:

Trim off the green ends of the beets. Wash thoroughly and cut into thin slices. Place in a deep pot and add water enough to cover. Bring it to a boil over medium-high heat and cook for 15-20 minutes. Remove from the heat drain well. Set aside.

Heat up a non-stick skillet over medium-high heat. Add pumpkin seeds and stir-fry for 3-5 minutes, or until lightly toasted.

In a mixing bowl, combine Greek yogurt, sour cream, yellow mustard, and olive oil. Stir until combined and set aside.

Place the egg in a deep pot and add water enough to cover. Bring it to a boil over medium-high heat. Cook for 10-12 minutes. Remove from the heat and let it cool completely. Peel and chop into bite-sized pieces.

Now, combine beets, eggs, garlic, arugula, and pumpkin seeds. Add salt to taste and stir until well combined.

Pour over the yogurt mixture and stir once again before serving.

Enjoy!

Nutritional information per serving: Kcal: 265, Protein: 12.9g, Carbs: 13.7g, Fats: 19.1g

14. Lentil Tomato Salad

Ingredients:

1 cup lentils, drained

1 large Roma tomato, chopped

1 small Jalapeno pepper, finely chopped

1 garlic clove, minced

1 medium-sized cucumber, chopped

1 medium-sized purple onion, chopped

1 large red bell pepper, chopped

1 tbsp. olive oil

¼ tsp. cumin, ground

1 tbsp. lemon juice, freshly squeezed

Preparation:

Rinse the tomato and remove the stem. Chop into bite-sized pieces and set aside.

Wash the bell pepper and cut lengthwise in half. Remove the stem and seeds. Cut into bite-sized pieces and set aside.

Cut the cucumber into bite-sized pieces and set aside.

Peel the onion and chop into small pieces. Set aside.

Preheat the oil in a large saucepan over medium-high heat. Add garlic and Jalapeno pepper. Stir-fry for 2-3 minutes, or until golden.

Add lentils and sprinkle with cumin powder. Stir well and remove from the heat. Let it chill for a while and then transfer to a large bowl.

Now, add all vegetables to the bowl and drizzle with lemon juice. Toss to combine and serve immediately.

Nutritional information per serving: Kcal: 326, Protein: 18.8g, Carbs: 52.3g, Fats: 5.9g

15. Caesar Salad

Ingredients:

4 oz. chicken filets, skinless and boneless, cut into 1-inch thick strips

½ medium-sized tomato, chopped

1 egg, hard-boiled

¼ cup croutons

1 small cucumber, sliced

1 cup Iceberg lettuce

2 tbsp. Greek yogurt

1 tbsp. goat's cheese, crumbled

1 tbsp. olive oil

Salt and pepper to taste

Preparation:

Rinse the chicken under cold running water and pat-dry with a kitchen paper. Transfer to a cutting board and cut into bite-sized pieces. Set aside.

Preheat the oil in a medium saucepan over medium-high

heat. Add chicken and sprinkle with some salt and pepper to taste. Cook for 5 minutes, or until golden brown and crispy on the edges. Remove from the heat and set aside.

In a small mixing bowl, combine Greek yogurt, goat's cheese, olive oil, salt, and pepper. Mix until well combined and set aside.

Place the egg in a deep pot and add enough water to cover. Bring to a boil and cook for 12 minutes. Remove from the heat and rinse with ice cold water. Peel and chop into bite-sized pieces.

Now, combine chicken, tomato, croutons, cucumber, and lettuce in a large bowl. Drizzle with previously prepared dressing and stir well.

Serve immediately.

Nutritional information per serving: Kcal: 309, Protein: 15.7g, Carbs: 19g, Fats: 19.4g

16. Spicy Avocado Couscous Salad

Ingredients:

1 ripe avocado, cut into bite-sized pieces

½ cup couscous

1 tbsp. parsley, finely chopped

½ cup canned lentils, rinsed and drained

1 tbsp. canned corn, drained and rinsed

1 large red bell pepper, chopped

3 tbsp. olive oil

1 small chili pepper, seeded

1 garlic clove

½ tsp. salt

½ tsp. smoked paprika

Preparation:

Place the couscous in a deep bowl and pour in 1 cup of boiling water. Cover with a lid and let it stand for 10 minutes.

Meanwhile, combine olive oil, chili pepper, garlic, salt, and smoked paprika in a food processor. Blend until smooth and pureed. Optionally, add bell pepper instead chili if it is too spicy for your taste.

Fluff the couscous with a fork and add lentils along with avocado, corn, parsley, corn, and bell pepper.

Finally, drizzle with sauce and give it a good stir.

Serve immediately.

Nutritional information per serving: Kcal: 323, Protein: 9.3g, Carbs: 36.4g, Fats: 17g

17. Shiitake Spinach Salad

Ingredients:

1 cup Shiitake mushrooms, chopped

2 cups fresh baby spinach, roughly chopped

¼ cup Feta cheese, crumbled

1 garlic clove, minced

2 small beets, sliced

1 small onion, sliced

1 tsp. fresh thyme, ground

2 tbsp. olive oil

½ tbsp. balsamic vinegar

Salt and pepper to taste

Preparation:

Preheat the oil in a large saucepan over medium-high heat. Add garlic and onions. Stir-fry for 3-4 minutes, or until translucent.

Add mushrooms and sprinkle with some thyme, salt, and pepper to taste. Cook for 3-4 minutes, or until slightly soften.

Throw in the spinach and stir well. Cook for 2-3 minutes more and sprinkle with balsamic vinegar. Stir well and remove from the heat.

Transfer all to a large salad bowl and top with sliced beets, onions, and cheese.

Serve immediately.

Nutritional information per serving: Kcal: 278, Protein: 6.9g, Carbs: 26g, Fats: 18.5g

18. Potato Salad with Creamy Dressing

Ingredients:

2 medium-sized potatoes, cut into bite-sized pieces

1 large red bell pepper, chopped

1 small cucumber, sliced

¼ cup spring onions, chopped

1 tsp. yellow mustard

4 tbsp. Greek yogurt

1 tsp. white wine vinegar

¼ tsp. black pepper, ground

½ tsp. salt

Preparation:

Place the potatoes in a deep pot and add enough water to cover. Bring to a boil over medium-high heat. Cook for 10-15 minutes, or until fork-tender. Remove from the heat and drain. Set aside.

In a small mixing bowl, combine Greek yogurt, white wine vinegar, yellow mustard, black pepper, and salt. Mix until well combined and set aside.

Now, place the potatoes in a salad bowl and drizzle over with yogurt dressing. Sprinkle with green onions before serving.

Enjoy!

Nutritional information per serving: Kcal: 202, Protein: 6.5g, Carbs: 45.1g, Fats: 0.8g

19. Simple Tomato Mozzarella Salad

Ingredients:

2 large tomatoes, cut into bite-sized pieces

½ cup Mozzarella cheese, sliced

½ small purple onion, finely chopped

¼ cup olives, pitted

2 tbsp. fresh parsley, finely chopped

½ tsp. dried oregano, ground

1 tbsp. extra-virgin olive oil

¼ tsp. sea salt

¼ tsp. black pepper

Preparation:

Rinse the tomatoes and cut into bite-sized pieces. Transfer to a salad bowl and add mozzarella cheese.

In a small mixing bowl, combine olive oil, dried oregano, sea salt, and black pepper. Mix until combined.

Drizzle the prepared salad with the dressing.

Sprinkle with parsley and top with olives before serving.

Enjoy!

Nutritional information per serving: Kcal: 285, Protein: 8.2g, Carbs: 21.3g, Fats: 21g

20. Bean Salad With Feta and Chia Seeds

Ingredients:

½ cup canned beans, drained and rinsed

1 small red onion, chopped

1 garlic clove, finely chopped

1 large tomato, chopped

¼ cup Feta cheese, crumbled

4 tsp. chia seeds

1 tsp. shallots, finely chopped

1 tbsp. fresh parsley, finely chopped

1 tsp. apple cider vinegar

1 tsp. yellow mustard

2 tbsp. olive oil

¼ tsp. cumin, ground

¼ tsp. dried oregano, ground

½ tsp. salt

¼ tsp. black pepper, ground

Preparation:

In a small mixing bowl, combine olive oil, apple cider vinegar, garlic, cumin, oregano, salt and pepper. Mix until well combined and set aside.

Place the beans in a large colander. Rinse under cold running water. Drain and transfer to a serving bowl.

Add tomato and onion. Drizzle with previously prepared mixture and give it a good stir.

Sprinkle with chia seeds and serve immediately.

Enjoy!

Nutritional information per serving: Kcal: 218, Protein: 4.8g, Carbs: 11.1g, Fats: 18.6g

21. Pepper Salad with Lentils

Ingredients:

4 large red bell peppers

½ cup lentils, drained

1 tbsp. fresh parsley, finely chopped

1 tbsp. fresh basil, finely chopped

1 tsp. fresh mint, finely chopped

¼ cup Feta cheese, cut into small cubes

2 tsp. balsamic vinegar

2 tbsp. olive oil

¼ tsp. cumin, ground

2-3 walnuts, chopped

¼ tsp. cayenne pepper

Preparation:

Preheat one tablespoon of olive oil in a large skillet over medium-high heat. Add peppers and sprinkle with some salt to taste. Cook for 3-4 minutes on each side, or until tender.

Rinse the lentils using a colander. Drain well and set aside.

Now, combine the remaining oil, balsamic vinegar, cumin, cayenne pepper, parsley, basil, and mint in a mixing bowl. Stir until well combined.

Combine peppers, lentils, and Feta cheese on a serving dish. Drizzle all with previously prepared dressing.

Top with walnuts and serve immediately.

Enjoy!

Nutritional information per serving: Kcal: 218, Protein: 4.8g, Carbs: 11.1g, Fats: 18.6g

22. Carrot Mustard Salad

Ingredients:

4 large carrots

1 tsp. yellow mustard

1 tsp. lemon juice, freshly squeezed

1 tbsp. olive oil

2 tbsp. fresh parsley, finely chopped

¼ tsp. dried thyme, ground

Salt and pepper

Preparation:

Rinse the carrot and gently peel the outer skin. Cut into thin slices and transfer to a salad bowl. Set aside.

In a small mixing bowl, combine yellow mustard, lemon juice, olive oil, and thyme. Add salt and pepper according to your taste. Mix until combined and drizzle over the carrots.

Give it a good stir and let it stand for 30 minutes before serving.

Enjoy!

Nutritional information per serving: Kcal: 246, Protein: 2.9g, Carbs: 29.4g, Fats: 14.3g

23. Tuna Rice Salad

Ingredients:

½ brown rice

4 oz. minced tuna, drained

1 tbsp. orange juice, freshly squeezed

½ fresh lemon, juiced

1 tbsp. fresh parsley, finely chopped

½ tsp. Italian seasoning

1 tbsp. drained capers

¼ cup olives, chopped

¼ tsp. smoked paprika, ground

¼ tsp. salt

1 tbsp. olive oil

Preparation:

In a small mixing bowl, combine olive oil, Italian seasoning, capers, olives, smoked paprika, and salt.

Place the rice in a heavy-bottomed pot. Add 1 ½ cup of water and bring it to a boil over medium-high heat. Cook for about 10-15 minutes, or until almost all the liquid has been absorbed.

Add lemon juice and orange juice. Give it a good stir and remove from the heat. Set aside to chill completely.

Transfer the rice to a serving bowl and add tuna and parsley. Drizzle with previously prepared mixture and stir well.

Serve immediately.

Nutritional information per serving: Kcal: 370, Protein: 19.2g, Carbs: 40g, Fats: 15.1g

24. Broccoli Lentil Salad

Ingredients:

2 cups fresh broccoli, chopped

½ cup lentils, soaked overnight

¼ cup spring onions, chopped

2 tbsp. parsley, finely chopped

1 garlic clove, minced

1 tsp. Dijon mustard

1 tsp. maple syrup

1 tbsp. olive oil

1 tbsp. apple cider vinegar

¼ tsp. black pepper

½ salt

Preparation:

Drain the lentils and place in a deep pot. Add two cups of water and bring it to boil. Cook for 20 minutes. Remove from the heat and drain well. Set aside.

Rinse the broccoli under cold running water using a large

colander. Drain and chop into bite-sized pieces. Steam for 10 minutes, or until tender.

In a small mixing bowl, combine parsley, Dijon mustard, maple syrup, olive oil, apple cider vinegar, pepper, and salt. Mix until well combined.

In a large salad bowl, combine lentils and broccoli. Drizzle with previously prepared dressing and give it a good stir.

Serve immediately.

Nutritional information per serving: Kcal: 370, Protein: 19.2g, Carbs: 40g, Fats: 15.1g

25. Sesame Chicken Salad

Ingredients:

4 oz. chicken breast, skinless and boneless

½ small onion, chopped

2 tsp. soy sauce

½ tsp. dried rosemary, ground

½ cup cherry tomatoes, chopped

¼ cup cottage cheese

1 tsp. sesame seeds

1 tsp. balsamic vinegar

2 cups Romaine lettuce, roughly chopped

1 tbsp. olive oil

Salt to taste

Preparation:

Rinse the chicken under running water and pat-dry with a kitchen paper. Transfer to a cutting board and cut into strips. Generously brush with soy sauce and sprinkle with rosemary. Let it sit for 10 minutes to allow spices to penetrate into the meat.

Preheat the oil in a skillet over medium-high heat. Add chicken and cook for 5 minutes, or until golden brown.

In a large salad bowl, combine lettuce, cheese, and cherry tomatoes. Top with meat and sprinkle all with sesame seeds and balsamic vinegar.

Add some salt to taste. However it's optional.

Enjoy!

Nutritional information per serving: Kcal: 371, Protein: 34.7g, Carbs: 14.1g, Fats: 19.9g

26. Beet Salad with Leeks

Ingredients:

2 large beets, chopped into bite-sized pieces

1 cup leeks, chopped

1 large carrot, sliced

1 garlic clove, minced

1 cup Greek yogurt

½ tsp. dried thyme

½ whole lemon, juiced

½ tsp. black pepper

Salt

1 tbsp. olive oil

Preparation:

Rinse the beet well and trim off the green parts. Place it in a deep pot and add water enough to cover. Bring it to a boil and cook for 20 minutes. Remove from the heat and drain. Let it cool completely and chop into bite-sized pieces.

Preheat the oil in a skillet over medium-high heat. Add

carrots and cook for 5 minutes, stirring occasionally. Add leeks and garlic. Pour in some water to help the cooking process. Stir-fry for about 10-15 minutes, or until the leeks are tender.

In a small mixing bowl, combine Greek yogurt, lemon juice, thyme, pepper, and salt. Mix until well combined.

Now, combine cooked beets, carrots, and leeks in a salad bowl. Drizzle over with yogurt dressing and give it a good stir.

Serve immediately.

Nutritional information per serving: Kcal: 332, Protein: 25.8g, Carbs: 49.6g, Fats: 4.8g

27. Sweet Potato Kale Salad with Sesame Seeds

Ingredients:

1 medium-sized sweet potato, chopped

2 cups fresh kale, chopped

1 tsp. apple cider vinegar

1 tsp. avocado oil

1 tsp. sesame seeds

1 garlic clove, minced

Salt and pepper to taste

Preparation:

Peel and wash the potato. Cut into bite-sized pieces and transfer to a large pot. Add water enough to cover and sprinkle with some salt. Bring to a boil over medium-high heat. Cook for 5 minutes and turn off the heat. Cover with a lid and let it stand in hot water.

Using a large colander, rinse the kale under running water. Drain and torn into small pieces.

Preheat the oil in a saucepan over medium-high heat. Add garlic and cook for 2-3 minutes. Now, add kale and continue to cook for 3-4 minutes, or until wilted. Remove from the heat and set aside.

In a large salad bowl, combine sweet potato and kale. Drizzle with apple cider vinegar and sprinkle with sesame seeds. Give it a good stir and serve immediately.

Nutritional information per serving: Kcal: 198, Protein: 7.1g, Carbs: 39.6g, Fats: 2.3g

28. Watercress Mango Salad with Pomegranate Seeds

Ingredients:

2 cups watercress, chopped

1 ripe mango, chopped

¼ cup pomegranate seeds

1 tbsp. walnuts, chopped

1 orange, freshly juiced

½ lemon, freshly juiced

3 tsp. hemp oil

1 tsp. honey

Salt and pepper to taste

Preparation:

Using a large colander, rinse the watercress under cold running water. Drain and set aside.

Peel the mango and chop into bite-sized pieces. Set aside.

In a small mixing bowl, combine orange juice, lemon juice, hemp oil, honey, salt, and pepper. Mix until well combined and set aside.

In a salad bowl, combine watercress and mango. Drizzle with previously prepared dressing and give it a good stir.

Top with pomegranate seeds and walnuts before serving.

Nutritional information per serving: Kcal: 198, Protein: 7.1g, Carbs: 39.6g, Fats: 2.3g

29. Spicy Orange Cumin Salad

Ingredients:

3 large oranges, peeled

1 small red onion, chopped

2 tsp. olive oil

¼ cup olives, pitted

1 whole lime, juiced

½ tsp. black pepper, ground

½ tsp. black cumin powder

Preparation:

Peel the orange and divide into wedges. Set aside.

Peel the onions and cut into thin slices along with olives.

In a small mixing bowl, combine lime juice, pepper, and cumin powder. Mix until well combined. Set aside.

Now, combine orange, onions, and olives in a salad bowl. Drizzle with previously prepared dressing.

Optionally, top with finely chopped coriander leaves or basil.

Serve immediately.

Nutritional information per serving: Kcal: 244, Protein: 3.2g, Carbs: 47.1g, Fats: 6.9g

30. Cauliflower Broccoli Salad with Dried Cranberries

Ingredients:

2 cups cauliflower, chopped

2 cups broccoli, chopped

1 tbsp. dried cranberries

1 tbsp. almond flakes

1 tsp. Dijon mustard

1 whole lemon, juiced

2 garlic cloves, minced

1 tsp. avocado oil

½ tsp. black pepper, ground

½ tsp. salt

Preparation:

Line a small baking sheet with some parchment paper. Spread the almond flakes evenly in one layer. Place it in the oven and bake for 2 minutes at 450 degrees. Remove from the oven and let it cool completely.

Rinse the cauliflower and broccoli using a large colander.

Chop into bite-sized pieces and place in a large bowl. Add cranberries and toasted almonds and set aside.

In a small mixing bowl, combine Dijon mustard, lemon juice, garlic, avocado oil, pepper, and salt. Mix until combined and drizzle the salad. Give it a good stir and serve immediately.

Enjoy!

Nutritional information per serving: Kcal: 291, Protein: 15.1g, Carbs: 29g, Fats: 14.7g

31. Creamy Tuna Tomato Salad

Ingredients:

1 large tomato, chopped

4 oz. canned tuna, drained

1 large green bell pepper, chopped

1 small cucumber, cubed

1 cup Greek yogurt

1 tsp. apple cider vinegar

1 tsp. pine nuts

1 tbsp. extra-virgin olive oil

Salt and pepper to taste

Preparation:

Wash the tomato and chop into bite-sized pieces. Place in a large salad bowl and set aside.

Cut the pepper lengthwise into halves. Remove the stem and seeds. Chop into small pieces and add to the bowl.

Wash the cucumber and cut into small cubes. Add to the bowl and set aside.

Now, combine yogurt, vinegar, pine nuts, and olive oil in a small mixing bowl. Add salt and pepper according to your taste and mix well.

Drizzle the creamy dressing over the salad and give it a good stir. Add more salt and pepper if needed.

Serve immediately.

Nutritional information per serving: Kcal: 309, Protein: 27.7g, Carbs: 17.7g, Fats: 15.1g

32. Grape Tomato Avocado Salad with Greek Dressing

Ingredients:

1 cup grape tomatoes, chopped

1 small cucumber, chopped

½ ripe avocado, chopped

1 small purple onion, sliced

½ cup Feta cheese, crumbled

1 tbsp. fresh parsley, finely chopped

2 tbsp. olive oil

½ whole lemon, juiced

1 tsp. Dijon mustard

1 garlic clove, crushed

1 tsp. fresh basil, finely chopped

¼ tsp. dried oregano, ground

Salt to taste

Preparation:

In a mixing bowl, combine olive oil, fresh lemon juice, Dijon mustard, garlic, fresh basil, oregano, and salt. Mix until well combined and set aside.

Wash cucumber and cut into thin slices. Set aside.

Using a large colander, rinse the grape tomatoes under running water. Drain and cut each in half. Set aside.

Cut the avocado in half. Remove the pit and cut into thin slices. Reserve the rest in the refrigerator. Optionally, sprinkle with some lemon juice and set aside for 5 minutes.

Peel the onion and chop into small pieces.

Now, combine tomatoes, cucumber, avocado, and onion in a salad bowl. Drizzle all with previously prepared dressing and give it a gentle stir. Sprinkle all with fresh parsley and serve immediately.

Nutritional information per serving: Kcal: 253, Protein: 5.8g, Carbs: 12.6g, Fats: 21.5g

33. Smoked Trout Fusilli Salad

Ingredients:

3 oz. fusilli pasta

2 oz. smoked trout, thinly sliced

½ cup sour cream

2 large red bell peppers, chopped

½ tsp. dried dill, ground

½ whole lemon, juiced

1 tbsp. olive oil

Salt and pepper to taste

Preparation:

Place the pasta in a deep pot and water enough to cover. Bring to a boil over medium-high heat. Cook for 10-13 minutes. Remove from the heat and drain using a large colander. Rinse under cold running water and set aside.

Cut the bell peppers lengthwise into halves. Remove the stems and seeds. Chop into small pieces and set aside.

In a small bowl, combine sour cream, lemon juice, olive oil, salt, and pepper. Mix until well combined.

In a salad bowl, combine pasta, smoked trout, and bell peppers. Drizzle with prepared dressing and gently stir.

Optionally, garnish with some fresh parsley, or add a few olives before serving.

Enjoy!

Nutritional information per serving: Kcal: 288, Protein: 10.8g, Carbs: 29g, Fats: 14.9g

34. Mexican Potato Salad

Ingredients:

2 large potatoes, cut into cubes

1 large red bell pepper, chopped

¼ cup cheddar cheese, shredded

2 tbsp. red wine vinegar

1 tbsp. corn, rinsed and drained

½ cup spring onions, chopped

1 tbsp. fresh parsley, finely chopped

¼ cup Greek yogurt

2 tbsp. olive oil

½ whole lime, juiced

½ tsp. garlic powder

1 tsp. dried oregano, ground

¼ tsp. cumin powder

¼ tsp. chili powder

½ tsp. black pepper, ground

Salt

Preparation:

In a mixing bowl, combine Greek yogurt, olive oil, lime juice, garlic powder, oregano, cumin, chili powder, salt, and pepper. Mix until well combined and refrigerate.

Peel and wash the potatoes. Place in a deep pot and sprinkle with some salt. Add water enough to cover and bring to a boil over medium-high heat. Cook for 20 minutes, or until tender. Remove from the heat and drain. Set aside to cool completely. Chop into bite-sized cubes and set aside.

In a small bowl, combine salt and red wine vinegar. Mix until the salt has been dissolved. Drizzle over the potatoes and give it a good stir and set aside until all the liquid has been soaked up.

Now, add bell peppers and shredded cheddar cheese. Drizzle all with previously prepared yogurt mixture and gently stir.

Serve immediately.

Nutritional information per serving: Kcal: 278, Protein: 8.1g, Carbs: 40.9g, Fats: 10.4g

35. Eggplant Chermoula Salad

Ingredients:

2 medium-sized eggplants, sliced

2 tbsp. olive oil

1 garlic clove, minced

½ tsp. cumin powder

½ tsp. coriander powder

½ tsp. smoked paprika

1 tbsp. fresh parsley, finely chopped

1 tbsp. fresh cilantro, finely chopped

¼ cup fresh spring onions, chopped

1 tbsp. lemon juice, freshly squeezed

Salt

Preparation:

Preheat the oven to 400 degrees. Line some parchment paper over a baking sheet and set aside.

Rinse well the eggplants and pat-dry with a kitchen paper. Transfer to a cutting board and cut into thin slices using a sharp knife.

Spread the eggplant over a prepared baking sheet and bake for 20-25 minutes.

When done, remove from the oven and let it cool completely.

In a food processor, combine olive oil, garlic, cumin powder, coriander powder, smoked paprika, parsley, cilantro, spring onions, fresh lemon juice, and salt. Pulse until well incorporated.

Transfer the chilled eggplant to a serving dish and drizzle over with chermoula dressing.

Optionally, serve with some garlic toasted bread.

Enjoy!

Nutritional information per serving: Kcal: 269, Protein: 6g, Carbs: 34.5g, Fats: 15.3g

36. Zucchini Carpaccio Salad

Ingredients:

3 medium-sized zucchinis, thinly sliced

¼ cup Parmesan cheese, thinly sliced

2 tbsp. capers, drained

¼ cup black olives

1 whole lemon, freshly juiced

½ cup fresh mint, roughly chopped

3 tbsp. olive oil

1 tsp. apple cider vinegar

Salt and pepper to taste

Preparation:

Rinse and pat-dry the zucchinis. Using a sharp paring knife, cut thin lengthwise slices. Discard the middle parts with seeds.

Spread the zucchini slices in one layer over a large baking sheet. Sprinkle with salt, pepper, and vinegar. Set aside for 30 minutes.

Now, in a small mixing bowl, combine olive oil, lemon juice, salt, and pepper. Mix until well combined.

Transfer the zucchini to a serving bowl and drizzle with previously prepared dressing. Top with mint, capers, and cheese.

Stir once and serve immediately.

Enjoy!

Nutritional information per serving: Kcal: 304, Protein: 9.2g, Carbs: 13.8g, Fats: 26.6g

37. Roquefort Radish Salad with Raspberries

Ingredients:

2 cups fresh arugula, chopped

3 medium-sized radishes, sliced

½ cup Roquefort cheese, (or any other blue cheese you have on hand)

½ cup fresh raspberries

1 tbsp. walnuts, finely chopped

1 tbsp. olive oil

1 tsp. apple cider vinegar

¼ tsp. dried dill, ground

Salt and pepper

Preparation:

Using a large colander, rinse the arugula under cold running water. Drain and roughly torn with your hands. Transfer to a large salad bowl and set aside. Optionally, sprinkle with some lemon juice for some extra flavor.

Rinse the radishes and trim off the green parts. Cut into thin slices and add to the bowl with arugula.

Cut the cheese into small cubes and add to the salad.

Now, sprinkle all with olive oil, apple cider vinegar, dried dill, and salt. Give it a good stir and top with raspberries and walnuts.

Serve immediately.

Nutritional information per serving: Kcal: 226, Protein: 9.1g, Carbs: 5.8g, Fats: 19.3g

38. Asparagus Strawberry Salad

Ingredients:

5 oz. asparagus, trimmed and chopped

6 oz. strawberries, chopped

¼ cup raspberries

1 tbsp. balsamic vinegar

1 tbsp. olive oil

Salt and pepper

Preparation:

In a food processor, combine raspberries, balsamic vinegar, olive oil, salt, and pepper. Pulse until smooth and set aside.

Rinse and drain the asparagus. Trim off the woody ends and cut into bite-sized pieces. Transfer to a deep pot and add enough water to cover. Bring to a boil over medium-high heat. Cook for 2 minutes and remove from the heat. Drain and set aside to cool completely.

Using a large colander, rinse well the strawberries. Drain and remove the stems. Chop into bite-sized pieces.

Now, combine asparagus and strawberries in a large bowl.

Drizzle with previously prepared sauce and give it a good stir.

Serve immediately.

Nutritional information per serving: Kcal: 222, Protein: 4.6g, Carbs: 22.4g, Fats: 14.9g

39. Creamy Cucumber Salad

Ingredients:

2 cups Greek yogurt

2 medium-sized cucumbers, finely chopped

2 garlic cloves, minced

¼ cup fresh dill, finely chopped

2 tbsp. extra-virgin olive oil

1 tbsp. walnuts, finely chopped

Salt and pepper to taste

Preparation:

Wash the cucumbers and chop into small pieces. Place in a large salad bowl and set aside.

In a small bowl, garlic, fresh dill, olive oil, salt, and pepper. Mix until well incorporated and pour over the cucumbers. Mix once and set aside for 15 minutes to allow flavors to merge.

Now, add Greek yogurt and stir until all well combined. Top with walnuts before serving.

Optionally, add some cayenne pepper or chili for some

extra flavor.

Enjoy!

Nutritional information per serving: Kcal: 360, Protein: 24.5g, Carbs: 23.7g, Fats: 20.9g

40. Greek Lentil Salad

Ingredients:

½ cup lentils, soaked overnight

1 small purple onion, chopped

1 small cucumber, chopped

½ cup cherry tomatoes, halved

¼ cup Kalamata olives

¼ cup Feta cheese, cubed

1 tsp. fresh dill, finely chopped

2 tbsp. olive oil

1 garlic clove, crushed

¼ tsp. dried oregano, ground

1 tbsp. lemon juice, freshly squeezed

Salt and pepper to taste

Preparation:

In a small mixing bowl, combine olive oil, garlic, dried oregano, lemon juice, salt, and pepper. Mix until well combined and set aside.

Drain the lentils and place in a deep pot. Add 2 cups of water and a pinch of salt. Bring to a boil over medium-high heat. Cook for 20 minutes and remove from the heat. Drain well and rinse under cold water to chill. Set aside.

Wash and prepare the vegetables.

In a large salad bowl, combine onions, cucumber, cherry tomatoes, Kalamata olives, and Feta cheese. Add lentils and stir once.

Now, drizzle with previously prepared dressing and stir well.

Serve immediately.

Nutritional information per serving: Kcal: 273, Protein: 11.5g, Carbs: 28.1g, Fats: 13.8g

41. Broccoli Salad with Raisins

Ingredients:

2 cups broccoli, chopped

1 small purple onion, finely chopped

1 tbsp. raisins

½ cup cheddar cheese, cut into cubes

½ cup cherry tomatoes, halved

2 tsp. apple cider vinegar

1 tbsp. olive oil

Salt and pepper

Preparation:

Using a large colander, rinse the broccoli under cold running water. Chop into bite-sized pieces and set aside.

Peel the onion and finely chop. Set aside.

Rinse the cherry tomatoes and remove the stems. Cut each tomato in half and set aside. In case you use the regular tomato, remove the seeds and cut into small pieces.

Now, combine broccoli, onion, tomatoes, raisins, and

cheddar cheese in a large salad bowl. Sprinkle all with apple cider vinegar, olive oil, salt, and pepper.

Mix until all well incorporated and serve immediately.

Nutritional information per serving: Kcal: 242, Protein: 10.5g, Carbs: 15.1g, Fats: 16.8g

42. Classic Waldorf Salad

Ingredients:

2 large Granny Smith's apple, cored

2 large celery sticks

1 cup Greek yogurt

½ whole lemon, juiced

1 tbsp. walnuts, minced

Salt and pepper to taste

Parsley

Preparation:

Wash the apples and cut lengthwise in half. Remove the core and cut into thin slices or strips. Set aside.

Rinse the celery and discard the leaves. Cut each stick into 1-inch thick strips. Set aside.

In a mixing bowl, combine Greek yogurt, lemon, salt, and pepper. Mix until well incorporated and set aside.

Now, combine apples and celery in a salad bowl. Add yogurt mixture and stir until all well combined.

Top with walnuts and garnish with parsley.

Enjoy!

Nutritional information per serving: Kcal: 226, Protein: 11.6g, Carbs: 37.2g, Fats: 4.7g

43. Green Bean Fusilli Salad

Ingredients:

4 oz. fusilli pasta

1 cup green beans

¼ cup Feta cheese, crumbled

¼ cup olives, pitted and chopped

2 garlic cloves, minced

½ onion, finely chopped

1 cup yogurt, low-fat

1 tsp. yellow mustard

2 tbsp. olive oil

½ tsp. dried dill, ground

½ tsp. red pepper, ground

Salt

Preparation:

Place the pasta in a deep pot. Add enough water to cover and bring it to a boil. Sprinkle with some salt and cook for 10 minutes over medium-high heat. Remove from the heat and transfer to a large colander. Rinse under cold running water and set aside.

Place the green beans in a deep pot and cover with water. Bring to a boil over medium-high heat and cook for 5 minutes. Remove from the heat and drain. Set aside.

Preheat one tablespoon of olive oil in a large skillet over medium-high heat. Add onions and garlic. Stir-fry for 2-3 minutes, or until translucent. Add green beans and cook for 5 minutes. Remove from the heat and transfer to a large salad bowl.

Add pasta to the bowl and stir well. Set aside.

Now, combine the remaining olive oil, yogurt, mustard, dried dill, red pepper, and a pinch of salt in a mixing bowl. Mix until well combined and pour over prepared beans and pasta. Top with olives and cheese before serving.

Enjoy!

Nutritional information per serving: Kcal: 264, Protein: 9.3g, Carbs: 31.5g, Fats: 11.2g

44. Cooked Celery Salad

Ingredients:

4 celery sticks, with leaves

1 whole lemon, juiced

3 tbsp. walnuts, halved

1 small purple onion, finely chopped

2 tbsp. white wine vinegar

2 cups lamb's lettuce, roughly chopped

1 tsp. flaxseed oil

½ tsp. salt

½ tsp. black pepper, ground

Preparation:

Rinse the celery under cold running water and drain. Transfer to a cutting board and separate sticks and leaves. Chop the sticks into strips and finely chop the leaves. Set aside.

Transfer the celery sticks in a deep pot. Cover with water and bring to a boil over medium-high heat. Cook for 8 minutes. Add celery leaves and fresh lemon juice. Stir once and cook for 2-3 minutes more. Remove from the heat and drain. Rinse all under cold running water immediately. Set aside.

In a mixing bowl, combine onions, vinegar, salt, and pepper. Mix until well incorporated. Add flaxseed oil and mix again until combined.

Now, arrange the lamb's lettuce over a serving dish and top with celery. Drizzle with previously prepared dressing.

Serve cold.

Nutritional information per serving: Kcal: 273, Protein: 8.8g, Carbs: 17.9g, Fats: 19g

45. Avocado Egg Salad

Ingredients:

1 ripe avocado, cut into cubes

2 large eggs, hard-boiled

2 spring onions, chopped

½ cup Greek yogurt

1 tbsp. sour cream

1 whole lime, juiced

1 tsp. fresh thyme, finely chopped

Salt and pepper to taste

Preparation:

Place the eggs in a deep pot. Add water enough to cover and bring to a boil over medium-high heat. Cook for 10-12 minutes. Remove from the heat and transfer to a bowl with ice cold water. You can add a few ice cubes to speed up the process. Peel and cut into bite-sized pieces. Set aside.

Peel the avocado and cut lengthwise in half. Remove the pit and cut into bite-sized cubes. Set aside.

In a mixing bowl, combine Greek yogurt, sour cream, lime

juice, thyme, salt, and pepper. Mix until combined.

In a serving bowl, combine eggs and avocado. Drizzle with previously prepared dressing and give it a good stir.

Serve immediately.

Nutritional information per serving: Kcal: 343, Protein: 14g, Carbs: 16.3g, Fats: 27g

46. Grilled Mustard Turkey Salad

Ingredients:

8 oz. turkey breast, skinless and boneless

1 tbsp. yellow mustard

3 tsp. olive oil

½ tsp. salt

½ tsp. black pepper, ground

2 cups Romaine lettuce, chopped

1 cup lamb's lettuce

½ cup cherry tomatoes, chopped

1 tbsp. Parmesan cheese, shredded

2 tsp. red wine vinegar

Preparation:

Rinse and drain the turkey breast. Transfer to a cutting board and cut into thin slices. Set aside.

In a small mixing bowl, combine 2 teaspoons of olive oil, salt, black pepper, and mustard. Mix until combined and pour over the meat. Rub with your hands to allow flavors to penetrate into the meat. Cover the dish with a plastic foil and refrigerate for 1 hour.

Preheat the grill to medium-high. Add meat and grill for 3-4 minutes on each side. Remove from the heat and transfer to a cutting board. Let it chill for a while and then cut into strips.

Wash and prepare the vegetables.

In a large salad bowl, combine lettuce, lamb's lettuce, and cherry tomatoes. Top with turkey strips and drizzle with red wine vinegar. Sprinkle with parmesan cheese and serve immediately.

Nutritional information per serving: Kcal: 248, Protein: 25g, Carbs: 9.6g, Fats: 12.4g

47. Shrimp Avocado Salad

Ingredients:

4 oz. shrimps, cleaned and deveined

½ ripe avocado, chopped

¼ cup Feta cheese, crumbled

1 medium-sized green bell pepper, chopped

½ cup cherry tomatoes, chopped

½ cup fresh mint, roughly chopped

1 small purple onion, chopped

¼ cup green olives, pitted

1 tbsp. fresh parsley, finely chopped

1 whole lime, juiced

¼ tsp. garlic powder

¼ tsp. dried oregano, ground

½ tsp. red pepper flakes

2 tbsp. olive oil

Salt to taste

Preparation:

In a small mixing bowl, combine lime juice, oregano, garlic, 1 tablespoon of olive oil, pepper flakes, and salt. Mix until well combined and set aside.

Wash and prepare the vegetables.

In a large salad bowl, combine cherry tomatoes, mint, purple onion, green olives, and parsley. Drizzle with previously prepared dressing and refrigerate for 20 minutes.

Preheat the remaining oil in a skillet over medium-high heat. Add shrimps and sprinkle with some salt and red pepper. Cook for 2-3 minutes, or until set. Remove from the heat and set aside to chill for a while.

Now, add cheese and avocado to the salad. Mix again and top with shrimps. Garnish with fresh mint and serve immediately.

Enjoy!

Nutritional information per serving: Kcal: 264, Protein: 12.6g, Carbs: 12.2g, Fats: 19.6g

48. Chicken Celery Salad

Ingredients:

6 oz. chicken thighs, skinless and boneless

2 tbsp. dried cranberries

2 medium-sized celery sticks, chopped

4 spring onions, chopped

2 tbsp. Greek yogurt

1 tbsp. sour cream

1 tbsp. olive oil

½ tsp. dried oregano, ground

¼ tsp. dried thyme, ground

Salt and pepper to taste

Preparation:

Rinse the chicken under cold running water and pat-dry with a kitchen paper. Transfer to a cutting board and chop into bite-sized pieces.

Rinse the celery and discard the leaves. Cut the sticks into small pieces and set aside.

Rinse the spring onions and chop into small pieces. Set aside.

Preheat the oil in medium skillet over medium-high heat. Add chicken and sprinkle with some salt and pepper. Cook for 3-5 minutes, or until golden brown. Remove from the heat and set aside.

Now, combine chicken, celery, and spring onions in a large salad bowl.

In a small mixing bowl, combine Greek yogurt, sour cream, dried oregano, dried thyme, salt, and pepper. Mix until well combined and drizzle over the salad. Give it a good stir and serve immediately.

Optionally, garnish with lime or lemon slices.

Nutritional information per serving: Kcal: 275, Protein: 28.2g, Carbs: 5.6g, Fats: 15.2g

49. Butternut Squash Salad with Feta and Arugula

Ingredients:

2 cups butternut squash, cubed

¼ cup Feta cheese, crumbled

2 cups arugula, roughly chopped

1 tbsp. extra-virgin olive oil

½ tsp. salt

½ tsp. black pepper, ground

½ tsp. Italian seasoning

Preparation:

Preheat the oven to 350 degrees. Line some parchment paper over a baking sheet and set aside.

Cut the squash lengthwise in half. Using a tablespoon, scoop out the seeds and inner soft flesh. Peel and cut into bite-sized cubes. Fill the measuring cups and reserve the rest in the refrigerator.

Spread the squash over a prepared baking sheet. Sprinkle with some olive oil, salt, and Italian seasoning. Bake for about 30-40 minutes. Remove to a wire rack and let it chill completely.

Rinse the arugula under cold running water. Drain and roughly chop into small pieces.

Now, combine squash, arugula, and cheese in a salad bowl. Optionally, drizzle with some lemon juice and serve immediately.

Enjoy!

Nutritional information per serving: Kcal: 182, Protein: 4.6g, Carbs: 18.3g, Fats: 11.6g

ADDITIONAL TITLES FROM THIS AUTHOR

70 Effective Meal Recipes to Prevent and Solve Being Overweight: Burn Fat Fast by Using Proper Dieting and Smart Nutrition

By Joe Correa CSN

48 Acne Solving Meal Recipes: The Fast and Natural Path to Fixing Your Acne Problems in Less Than 10 Days!

By Joe Correa CSN

41 Alzheimer's Preventing Meal Recipes: Reduce or Eliminate Your Alzheimer's Condition in 30 Days or Less!

By Joe Correa CSN

70 Effective Breast Cancer Meal Recipes: Prevent and Fight Breast Cancer with Smart Nutrition and Powerful Foods

By Joe Correa CSN

www.ingramcontent.com/pod-product-compliance
Lightning Source LLC
Chambersburg PA
CBHW052102070526
44584CB00017B/2301